WEEKLY WR READER

EARLY LEARNING LIBRARY

How Plants Grow/Cómo crecen las plantas

How Tulips Grow/
Cómo crecen los tulipanes

by/por Joanne Mattern

Reading consultant/Consultora de lectura:
Susan Nations, M.Ed.,
author, literacy coach,
and consultant in literacy development/
autora, tutora de alfabetización,
y consultora de desarrollo de la lectura

Please visit our web site at: www.earlyliteracy.cc
For a free color catalog describing Weekly Reader® Early Learning Library's list
of high-quality books, call 1-877-445-5824 (USA) or 1-800-387-3178 (Canada).
Weekly Reader® Early Learning Library's fax: (414) 336-0164.

LLibrary of Congress Cataloging-in-Publication Data

Mattern, Joanne, 1963-
  [How tulips grow. (Spanish & English)]
  How tulips grow : Cómo crecen los tulipanes / Joanne Mattern.
    p. cm. — (How plants grow = Cómo crecen las plantas)
  Includes bibliographical references and index.
  ISBN 0-8368-6465-4 (library binding)
  ISBN 0-8368-6472-7 (softcover)
  1. Tulips—Growth—Juvenile literature. 2. Tulips—Development—Juvenile literature.
 I. Title: Cómo crecen los tulipanes. II. Title.
QK495.L72M3918   2006
584'.32—dc22   2005032368

This edition first published in 2006 by
Weekly Reader® Early Learning Library
A Member of the WRC Media Family of Companies
330 West Olive Street, Suite 100
Milwaukee, WI 53212 USA

Managing editor: Valerie J. Weber
Art direction: Tammy West
Cover design and page layout: Kami Strunsee
Translators: Tatiana Acosta and Guillermo Gutiérrez
Picture research: Cisley Celmer

Picture credits: Cover, © Jim Cummins/Taxi/Getty Images; p. 5 © SuperStock, Inc./SuperStock; pp. 7, 9, 19 © Michael Newman/PhotoEdit; p. 11 Kami Strunsee/© Weekly Reader® Early Learning Library; p. 13 © Chris R. Sharp/Photo Researchers, Inc.; p. 15 © Mike Comb/Science Photo Library/Photo Researchers, Inc.; p. 17 © Todd Gipstein/ National Geographic Society Image Collection; p. 21 © Martial Colomb/Photodisc Blue/Getty Images

Printed in the United States of America

1 2 3 4 5 6 7 8 9 10 09 08 07 06

Note to Educators and Parents

Reading is such an exciting adventure for young children! They are beginning to integrate their oral language skills with written language. To encourage children along the path to early literacy, books must be colorful, engaging, and interesting; they should invite the young reader to explore both the print and the pictures.

How Plants Grow is a new series designed to introduce young readers to the life cycle of familiar plants. In simple, easy-to-read language, each book explains how a specific plant begins, grows, and changes.

Each book is specially designed to support the young reader in the reading process. The familiar topics are appealing to young children and invite them to read — and reread — again and again. The full-color photographs and enhanced text further support the student during the reading process.

In addition to serving as wonderful picture books in schools, libraries, homes, and other places where children learn to love reading, these books are specifically intended to be read within an instructional guided reading group. This small group setting allows beginning readers to work with a fluent adult model as they make meaning from the text. After children develop fluency with the text and content, the book can be read independently. Children and adults alike will find these books supportive, engaging, and fun!

— Susan Nations, M.Ed., author, literacy coach,
and consultant in literacy development

Nota para los maestros y los padres

¡Leer es una aventura tan emocionante para los niños pequeños! A esta edad están comenzando a integrar su manejo del lenguaje oral con el lenguaje escrito. Para animar a los niños en el camino de la lectura incipiente, los libros deben ser coloridos, estimulantes e interesantes; deben invitar a los jóvenes lectores a explorar la letra impresa y las ilustraciones.

Cómo crecen las plantas es una nueva colección diseñada para presentar a los jóvenes lectores el ciclo de vida de plantas muy conocidas. Cada libro explica, en un lenguaje sencillo y fácil de leer, cómo nace, se desarrolla y cambia una planta específica.

Cada libro está especialmente diseñado para ayudar a los jóvenes lectores en el proceso de lectura. Los temas familiares llaman la atención de los niños y los invitan a leer — y releer — una y otra vez. Las fotografías a todo color y el tamaño de la letra ayudan aún más al estudiante en el proceso de lectura.

Además de servir como maravillosos libros ilustrados en escuelas, bibliotecas, hogares y otros lugares donde los niños aprenden a amar la lectura, estos libros han sido especialmente concebidos para ser leídos en un grupo de lectura guiada. Este contexto permite que los lectores incipientes trabajen con un adulto que domina la lectura mientras van determinando el significado del texto. Una vez que los niños dominan el texto y el contenido, el libro puede ser leído de manera independiente. ¡Estos libros les resultarán útiles, estimulantes y divertidos a niños y a adultos por igual!

— Susan Nations, M.Ed., autora, tutora de alfabetización, y
consultora de desarrollo de la lectura

See the pretty flowers!

These flowers are tulips.

¡Mira qué flores tan lindas!

Estas flores son tulipanes.

Tulips grow from bulbs. The
bulb holds food for the tulip.

——————————————————

Los tulipanes nacen de bulbos.
El bulbo contiene alimento
para el tulipán.

We plant tulips in the fall.

- - - - - - - - - - - - - - - - - -

Los tulipanes se plantan
en otoño.

9

In the winter, the bulb grows roots and a stem.

En el invierno, del bulbo nacen raíces y un tallo.

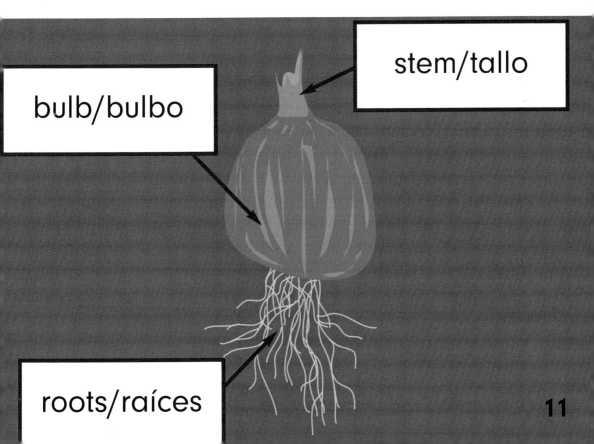

snow/nieve

stem/tallo

bulb/bulbo

roots/raíces

11

Spring is here! The tulip's stem grows out of the dirt. The bud on top holds leaves and a flower.

¡Ha llegado la primavera! El tallo del tulipán sale de la tierra. El capullo que ves arriba contiene hojas y una flor.

13

The leaves grow bigger. The bud opens into a flower.

Las hojas se hacen más grandes. El capullo se abre y se convierte en una flor.

15

Tulips come in so many colors!

¡Hay tulipanes de muchos colores!

In the fall, the flowers die. The bulb still lives underground.

En el otoño, las flores mueren. El bulbo sigue vivo bajo tierra.

In the spring, more tulips will bloom!

¡En la primavera, florecerán más tulipanes!

Glossary

bloom — to produce flowers

bud — part of a plant that grows into a flower or leaf

bulbs — underground parts from which some plants grow

stem — the part of a plant where leaves and flowers grow

Glosario

bulbos — partes que están bajo tierra y de las que brotan algunas plantas

capullo — parte de una planta que se convierte en una flor o una hoja

florecer — producir flores

tallo — parte de la planta de donde salen las hojas y las flores

For More Information/Más Información

Books

From Bulb to Flower. Dana Kababik (Lake Street Publishers)

Tulips. First Step Nonfiction (series). Melanie Mitchell
(Lerner Publications)

Libros

¿Cuál es tu flor favorita? (What's Your Favorite Flower?).
Allan Fowler (Children's Press)

Las flores/Flowers. Heinemann Lee Y Aprende/Heinemann
Read and Learn (series). Patricia Whitehouse (Heinemann)

Web Sites/Páginas web

Tulips: Color by Number
Tulipanes: Libro para colorear
www.littleexplorers.com/colorbynumber/tulips
This is a fun coloring and activity page about tulips.
Divertida página para colorear y con actividades sobre los tulipanes.

Index

Índice

About the Author

Joanne Mattern has written more than 150 books for children. Her favorite things to write about are animals, nature, history, sports, and famous people. Joanne also works in her local library. She lives in New York State with her husband, three daughters, and assorted pets. She enjoys animals, music, going to baseball games, reading, and visiting schools to talk about her books.

Información sobre la autora

Joanne Mattern ha escrito más de 150 libros para niños. Sus temas favoritos son los animales, la naturaleza, la historia, los deportes y la vida de personajes famosos. Además, Joanne trabaja en la biblioteca de su comunidad. Vive en el estado de Nueva York con su esposo, sus tres hijas y varias mascotas. A Joanne le gustan los animales, la música, ir al béisbol, leer y hacer visitas a las escuelas para hablar de sus libros.